A MATTE

A MATTER OF LIFE AND DEATH

based on the film by

Michael Powell and Emeric Pressburger

adapted by

Tom Morris and Emma Rice

OBERON BOOKS
LONDON

This adaptation first published in 2007 by Oberon Books Ltd
521 Caledonian Road, London N7 9RH
Tel: 020 7607 3637 / Fax: 020 7607 3629
e-mail: info@oberonbooks.com
www.oberonbooks.com

Quotation on page 32 is from 'I shall go the way of the open sea' by
Laurence Hope (pseudonym of Adela Florence Nicolson) (1865–1904)

Quotation on page 37 from 'The Knife' by Keith Douglas reproduced
by permission of Faber

Quotation on page 52 from 'How to Kill' by Keith Douglas
reproduced by permission of Faber

The words for Bellamy's song on pages 52–3 are from a poem by
F Officer M A Scott, whose papers are held in the Imperial War
Museum.

A catalogue record for this book is available from the British Library.

Cover design: National Theatre poster (photo by Steve Tanner)
designed by Michael Mayhew

ISBN: 1 84002 781 9 / 978-1-84002-781-5

Printed in Great Britain by Antony Rowe Ltd, Chippenham

Foreword

My Grandad was the gentlest human being I have ever met. He had a wide, clear face, snow-white hair and rough gardening hands as wide as shovels. He was as magnetic as catnip to the local cats as he stroked them so hard their tummies would dip down to the ground. As a child, I loved to be with him, calm and safe, picking runner beans or collecting sweet tomatoes from his greenhouse. My Grandad was also almost totally silent.

A lifelong campanologist, he carried a set of handbells with him throughout the war. He and his fellow soldiers would play them over the graves of the friends that had fallen.

I have talked to my family and now have a few more fragments to add to my own memories.

- Born in 1907, he left his home in Hampshire at 14 and walked to Dorset where he got a job working for the vicar of Evershot. He gardened and dug graves and learnt to ring the bells. He met my Gran, Edna Mary Rutley.
- He was enlisted into the Dorsetshire Regiment in 1939 along with all the other young men he had grown up with. He left my Gran with my mother, who was one year old, and pregnant with my uncle, whom he would not meet properly for another six years.
- In 1944 he was part of the second invasion, pushing forward through Holland and towards Arnhem. He was part of the battles dramatized in *A Bridge Too Far*.
- He described seeing bodies stacked at the side of the road like haystacks.
- My mother remembers him saying that after the war, he vowed he would enjoy every day.
- My uncle believes that if my Grandad had had the education and the support, he would have been a conscientious objector – if he'd met a German soldier, he would have shaken his hand.

So, this production of *A Matter of Life and Death* is dedicated to Harry Dennis Watton Bishop, my beloved Grandad, and all the memories he chose not to burden those he loved with. I thank him and all the other good men and women that fought with him for their bravery and their terror and the shadows they endured for the rest of their lives. It is in their honour that we will play Grandad's handbells in the performance. We will play them for the dead of all wars, thanking them, mourning them and raging against the dying of the light.

Emma Rice
2007

A longer version of this article appears in the National Theatre programme for *A Matter of Life and Death*.

This adaptation of *A Matter of Life and Death* was first performed on 3 May 2007 in the Olivier Theatre of the National Theatre, with the following company:

PETER, Tristan Sturrock
JUNE, Lyndsey Marshal
BOB, Craig Johnson
GIRL, Debbie Korley
DOC, Douglas Hodge
DR McEWEN, Andy Williams
MR ARCHER, Chiké Okonkwo
SGT BELLAMY, Mike Shepherd
BOY, Dan Canham
WOMAN, Dorothy Atkinson
NURSES, Fiona Chivers, Meryl Fernandes,
   Lorraine Stewart, Lizzie Winkler, Kirsty Woodward
INJURED AIRMEN, Jamie Bradley, Thomas Goodridge,
   Pieter Lawman, Róbert Luckay
CONDUCTOR, Gísli Örn Garðarsson
CHIEF RECORDER, Tamzin Griffin
FATHER, Stuart McLoughlin
MUSICIANS, Stu Barker, Pete Judge, Dominic Lawton,
   Alex Vann, Michael Vince

Director Emma Rice
Set Designer Bill Mitchell
Costume Designer Vicki Mortimer
Lighting Designer Mark Henderson
Choreographers Debra Batton, Emma Rice
Music Stu Barker
Sound Designer Gareth Fry
Projection Designers Jon Driscoll, Gemma Carrington

Characters

On Earth

PETER, a pilot
JUNE, a radio telephone operator
BOB, a wireless operator
GIRL
DR FRANK REEVES, 'DOC', a village doctor
DR PHIL McEWEN, an RAF doctor
MR ARCHER, an RAF surgeon
SGT BELLAMY, a wounded airman
SISTER

Between life and death

BOY
WOMAN
NURSES
INJURED AIRMEN

In the other world

CONDUCTOR 71
CHIEF RECORDER
SHAKESPEARE
FATHER
ACCOUNTANT
TWO ASSISTANTS
An ensemble of MUSICIANS

Note on characters and locations

In our version of the story, Peter is an English pilot and June is a WAAF radio telephone operator. June lives in Lee Wood House, near the beach, and operates the Air Traffic Control at the nearby Airfield on the East Anglian Coast. Peter is stationed with the RAF, at Killingholme, in Lincolnshire. Adjacent to Lee Wood House is the RAF hospital where Peter convalesces and has his operation. Dr Reeves lives and works in the village, five or six miles away.

Note on the text

This is the text of a devised show. We began with the screenplay of the original film. Some scenes were rewritten and taken into workshops at the National Studio where they were re-improvised and rewritten again. A new draft was taken into rehearsal, where many scenes were once again rewritten in response to the work of the acting and design company. Although some dialogue has been placed in square brackets to indicate that it is optional, this text is probably quite close to what will be spoken during the show's run at the National Theatre, but even then it will be subject to continual evolution and change and the occasional inspired improvisation on a nightly basis.

Tom Morris and Emma Rice
May 2007

SCENE 1

The stage is empty and vast. There is a canopy of stars high above.

A lone BOY walks to the centre. He looks around. He is not lost but neither is he at home. He looks to the audience, seems to understand the situation and smiles a distant smile.

A chorus of NURSES cycle on. They have black bicycles and crisp white uniforms. They seem to be waiting for something. They look up; check their pulses, their watches. They don't seem to be able to see our SOLDIER who watches the action. He sees them though, and follows their movements intently.

The NURSES notice something off to the right. They slowly walk away and in their wake follow a line of hospital beds... In their wake enters a chorus of young men. They are in pyjamas, holding books, poetry books; Byron and Marvell, Donne and Dickinson. They are INJURED SOLDIERS, AIRMEN and POETS.

They each go to a bed and pull back the covers. From inside the beds float out an entire solar system, all the planets glowing and turning. Our INJURED AIRMEN get into their beds and gaze up at the Milky Way in wonder.

Our lone BOY sits amongst the stars. He begins to speak in a relaxed voice.

BOY: This is the universe. Big isn't it? Thousands of suns. Myriads of stars. Separated by immense distances and by thin floating clouds of gas. The starlight makes the gas transparent. Where there are no stars it appears as dark obscuring clouds, like that great black cone over there.

Hello. There's a nova. A whole solar system exploded. Someone must have been messing about with the uranium atom. No. It's not our solar system I'm glad to say.

Ah. Those are called a 'globular cluster of stars'. Rather fine.

Down here in the right-hand corner. See that little chap rather like a boy scout's badge? It's a mass of gas expanding at thousands of miles a minute.

Ah. Here we are. We're getting nearer home. The moon. Our moon. In the first quarter. And here's the earth. Our earth. Moving around in its place. Part of the pattern. Part of the universe. Reassuring isn't it?

WOMAN: It's night over Europe. The night of the 2nd of May 1945. That tiny pin-point of fire is a burning city. It had a thousand-bomber raid an hour ago…

And this is what is called in England 'pea soup'. It rolled in from the channel overnight. I hope all our aircraft got home safely… Can you hear the fog-horns? Even big ships are frightened… And listen to the noises in the air…!

We hear radio noise and interference.

Listen. Radio messages, orders, distress signals – there's an SOS – bits of news.

We hear Churchill's voice.

Listen – Listen…!

The hospital beds ignite, flames licking angrily from beneath the covers. The AIRMEN begin to create a plane out of bicycles, ladders and bed sheets.

PETER CARTER is in the cockpit, trying desperately to radio the ground. To his left lies BOB. He is bloody and awkward, clearly dead. Two other airmen jump for safety, parachuting away from the burning plane. PETER is alone and doomed; a bubble of humanity in a picture of hell.

He holds a radio: two tin cans connected with red string. He throws one end into the air where it seems to fall for an eternity. JUNE, a wireless operator, chaotic and passionate, runs in and catches it.

JUNE: Request your position! Request your position! Come in Lancaster – come in Lancaster…

PETER: Position nil. Repeat nil. Age 27. Age 27. Got that?

Burst of interference.

It's very important! Education – interrupted. Violently interrupted. Religion Church of England. Politics – Conservative by nature, Labour by experience! What's your name?

Burst of interference.

JUNE: I cannot read you. Cannot read you. Request your position! Can you see our signal?

PETER: 'Reason thus with life:
If I do lose thee, I do lose a thing
That none but fools would keep:'

Burst of interference.

JUNE: Please repeat. I cannot read you.

PETER: 'Be absolute for death; either death or life
Shall thereby be the sweeter.'

Shakespeare wrote that. I'd rather have written that than flown through Hitler's legs!

Burst of interference.

JUNE: Cannot understand you! Hello, Lancaster! We are sending signals. Can you see our signals? Come in, Lancaster! Come in Lancaster!

PETER: 'But at my back I always hear
Time's winged chariot hurrying near;
And yonder all before us lie
Deserts of vast eternity.'

Andy Marvell. What a marvel! What's your name?

Burst of interference.

JUNE: Are you receiving me? Request your position! Come in, Lancaster!

PETER: I like your voice. I can't give you my position. Instruments gone. Crew gone too. Except Bob, my Sparks.

He's dead. The others baled out. On my orders. Time 03:35. Got that?

JUNE: Three crew dead. Three baled out – 03:35!

PETER: They'll be sorry about Bob. We all liked him.

Burst of interference.

JUNE: Hello! G George! Hello! G George! Are you alright? Are you going to try to land? Do you want a fix?

PETER: The name's not 'G for George', it's 'P for Peter'. Peter D Carter. D's for David. Squadron Leader Peter Carter. No, I'm not landing. Undercarriage is gone. Port engine's on fire. I am baling out presently. I am baling out. Take a telegram!

JUNE: Got your message! Received your message. We can hear you.

PETER: Telegram to my mother. Mrs Ray Carter, 88 Hampstead Lane, London, North West.

JUNE: 88 Hampstead Lane, London.

PETER: Tell her that I love her. You'll have to write it for me. What I want her to know is that I love her very much – that I've never shown it to her – not really – but that I've loved her always. Give love to my two sisters too. Don't forget them.

JUNE: Received your message. We can hear you. Are you wounded? Repeat. Are you wounded? Are you baling out?

PETER: What's your name?

JUNE: June.

PETER: June, I am baling out. I am baling out. But there's a catch. I've got no parachute.

Burst of interference.

JUNE: Hello! Hello Peter! Do not understand. Hello! Hello Peter. Can you hear me?

PETER: Hello June. Don't be afraid. It's quite simple. We've had it! And I'd rather jump than fry. After the first thousand feet what's the difference? I shan't know anything – I say – I hope I haven't frightened you?

JUNE: No! I'm not frightened.

PETER: Good.

JUNE: Your Sparks, you said he was dead. Hasn't he got a 'chute?

PETER: Cut to ribbons. Cannon-shell. June. Are you pretty?

JUNE: Not bad.

PETER: What's your favorite story?

JUNE: *The Wizard of Oz*

PETER: Best film ever! I wish I had my ruby slippers with me now.

JUNE: So do I.

PETER: Can you hear me as well as I hear you?

JUNE: Yes.

PETER: You have a good voice. You've got guts, too… It's funny. I've known dozens of girls – I was in love with some of them – but a girl whom I've never seen and never shall see, will hear my last words. I say, June, if you're around when they pick me up – turn your head away!

JUNE: No Peter!

We'll find somewhere you can try to land. Wait!

PETER: Don't go June. I'm badly on fire. She might break up at any minute. There's no way I could land.

JUNE: Let me try!

PETER: No. Let me do this in my own way. I want to be alone with you… Are you in love with anybody? No! Don't answer that!

JUNE: I could love a man like you, Peter.

PETER: I love you, June. You're Life and I'm leaving you! Where do you live? On the station?

JUNE: No. In a big country house. About five miles from here. Near the sea. Lee Wood House.

PETER: Old house?

JUNE: Yes. Very old.

PETER: Good. I'll be a ghost and come and see you. You aren't frightened of ghosts are you? It would be awful if you were.

JUNE: I'm not frightened.

PETER: What time will you be home.

JUNE: I'm on duty 'til six. I have breakfast in the mess. Then I have to cycle half an hour. I often go along the sands – oh, this is such nonsense!

PETER: No it isn't. It's the best sense I ever heard. I was lucky to get you, June. It can't be helped about the parachute. But I'll have wings soon anyway. Big white ones. I hope they haven't gone modern yet. I'd hate to have a propeller instead of wings. I say June.

JUNE: Yes.

PETER: Do you think there is anything after this? What do you think the Other world is like? I've got my own ideas –

JUNE: Oh – Peter…

PETER: I think it starts where this one leaves off; or where this one could leave off if we listened to Plato and Aristotle and Jesus; with all our little earthly problems solved but with greater problems worth the solving – I'll know soon enough. I'm signing off now June. Goodbye! Goodbye June.

Burst of interference.

JUNE: Hello G for George. Hello G George. Hello G George.

PETER throws his radio out of the plane and he prepares to jump. The tin can somersaults in the air.

PETER: 'The poet's eye in a fine frenzy rolling
Doth glance from heaven to earth, from earth to heaven.'

So long, Bob. I'll see you in a minute. You know what they wear by now. Propellor or wings…

PETER is alone and ready for death. He jumps into the cool air.

The tin can falls into JUNE's lap. She weeps.

Song

I didn't want to find you
  when I stepped outside the door.
I had no plan to meet you;
  I don't make plans anymore.
(Darling) please don't look behind you,
  Never mind what went before.
  It all hangs on the flip of a coin.

Come on dance the random tango;
  Will we fly or will we fall?
If we burn to dust and ashes
  Would it matter? Not at all.
If I didn't mean to chose you
Will it matter if I lose you?
When you dance the random tango
  You can fly above it all.

SCENE 2
THE PLACE YOU GO WHEN YOU DIE

All the dead are signing in a large register under the supervision of the CHIEF RECORDER. BOB enters, looking for PETER.

BOB: One…two…three nurses on bikes I'm in heaven.

RECORDER: Sergeant Trubshaw You can't wait here any longer. You must be mistaken about your captain.

BOB: This is the Aircrew Section, isn't it? Alright lads.

RECORDER: You should know.

BOB: He was due half an hour after me. This is his section. He hasn't reported. Either there's a mistake or he's AWOL.

RECORDER: Mistakes can't happen here.

BOB: He can't have got away with it! Mind you, oftentimes I'd be frozen on the plugs, you know: on my benders. But with Peter, it's 'muck you jack, I'm fireproof'! He'd fly that kite through soup to drop the cabbage. We called him the split-arsed king of crump. Sorry. It means daredevil.

RECORDER: I tell you there hasn't been a mistake here in a thousand years.

BOB: So there have been mistakes.

RECORDER: The girl before me – she was here six hundred and forty years –

BOB: Beep-bop-a-Lula!

RECORDER: – she said when the records don't balance – all the alarm bells start ringing in the Records Office.

BOB: I'll bet! Proper flap, eh? Out there?

RECORDER: Yes.

They look down into the records department. People are no bigger than ants and just as busy.

That's only the Living Records. Everyone on Earth has a file: Chinese or Russian, black or white, rich or poor, Republican or Democrat –

BOB: If anyone had told me that clerks are working away up here just like on Earth –

RECORDER: Everyone here is allowed to start how they like. There are millions of people on Earth who would think it heaven to be a clerk.

By the way. Don't say 'split-arsed king of crump'.

BOB: Quite so.

RECORDER: Try to behave with some kind of decorum.

BOB: Thanks for the gen, miss.

RECORDER: Sign here. Then come and get your wings.

She hands him his wings.

BOB: Do I get two? (*He points to his breast.*) Down there us Sparks only get one.

RECORDER: Everyone gets two. Please sign. You'll put the balance wrong unless you hurry up.

BOB: Okay! I don't want to start those bells ringing.

Hundreds of bells start ringing.

So – mistakes can't happen here, eh?

VOICE: Sergeant Trubshaw, you are to report to the office of the Chief Recorder.

BOB: Who's the Chief Recorder?

RECORDER: I am!

BOB: Well I'll be jaffered!

ACCOUNTANT: Deaths: Invoiced: 91,716; delivered: 91,715.

FIRST ASSISTANT: 91,716 invoiced – 91,715 checked in. Hmm.

SECOND ASSISTANT: The file of the missing man. Carter – Peter David.

FIRST ASSISTANT: Date of death: May the 2nd 1945. Time: 04:10.

RECORDER: Who was due to collect him?

SECOND ASSISTANT: Conductor 71.

RECORDER turns to another page in the book, looking for reference.

RECORDER: Conductor 71. Born, Bodo, Norway in 1911, known in life as Magnus the Magnificent. Profession – magician and illusionist.

Well? Conductor 71?

Where is he?

The CONDUCTOR enters through the audience, asking them to hide him. Perhaps trying to make himself invisible.

Eventually, RECORDER says:

Conductor 71. I can see you. Come here.

He tries to sneak out.

No. Come here! (*Etc.*)

How did you manage to lose Peter Carter?

CONDUCTOR: It was this English fog, madame.

RECORDER: Go on.

CONDUCTOR: It was so thick I couldn't see my own fingers. *Poof!* No aeroplane. Gone! Only fog.

The pilot jumped. He vanished in the fog. I missed him. It was impossible.

The CONDUCTOR mimes vanishing aeroplane. RECORDER Shuts him up.

RECORDER: Sergeant Trubshaw. You have been waiting all day for your pilot.

He nods to the CONDUCTOR.

BOB: I'm sorry I broke the rules. Sherbert dib-dab?

RECORDER: Thank you. (*To the CONDUCTOR.*) Nineteen hours and fifty minutes have elapsed. Don't you know that any slip must be reported immediately.

CONDUCTOR: I was trying to find him. I have been swimming about in this pea soup like a croûton.

RECORDER: Not long in the Service.

CONDUCTOR: Ten years.

RECORDER: Cause of death?

CONDUCTOR: Well…

She consults her book.

RECORDER: It says here you drowned in a bag of milk in the Empress Theatre in Frederikstad.

CONDUCTOR: It was a full house. In front of fifteen hundred people!

RECORDER: But that is not the question here, is it?

CONDUCTOR: No.

RECORDER: The question is, what has happened to Squadron Leader Peter Carter since 04:10 British Double Summer Time?

SCENE 3
THE BEACH

Far in the distance we see the body of a man. It is discarded on a beach with the sea lapping at its edges. He checks himself to see he is all there. He looks about, assuming he is dead.

PETER: Wonder whom I report to.

He sees a dog.

I always hoped there would be dogs.

The dog belongs to a little GIRL. She is wearing her favourite dress and has made a pair of wings from broken bicycle spokes.

21

Song

GIRL: (*Sings.*) Hold out your hand and I'll touch it.
Trust me. It isn't a dream.
If you've got the heart to believe it
Things can be more than they seem.

(You said)
Only believe that the clouds are high
Only believe that the sky is blue
Only believe and you'll wonder why
You didn't believe I'd come back to you.

PETER: Hello! Where do I go from here?

I'm new here. Just arrived. Where do I report? To get my wings?

GIRL: You mean the aerodrome?

PETER: Aerodrome?

They hear a plane flying overhead. PETER feels his body. He is alive.

Where am I?

The GIRL looks quizzical again.

This place – what's it called?

GIRL: The Burrows.

PETER: The Burrows – where?

GIRL: Lee Wood.

PETER: Lee Wood!

GIRL: Yes.

PETER: Do you know the big house – Lee Wood House.

GIRL: That's it. Where the smoke is behind those trees.

PETER: What's the shortest way?

GIRL: There's a track from the beach. See? See that bike?

PETER: Yes. Whose is it?

GIRL: Dunno. One of the radio operators from the aerodrome. They live up at the House. They –

JUNE is cycling along the beach. PETER sees her and runs towards her. He runs as if his life depends on it.

PETER: Hello! Hello! Stop! Hello!

She gets off her bike. She stands by it. They face each other. Looking for something they already know.

JUNE: Hello yourself. What's wrong?

PETER: June.

JUNE: Peter!

They throw themselves at each other, falling over on top of the bike, a mess of arms and legs, wheels and stocking tops. They almost devour each other. In their devouring, some of these words might be audible:

How did you get here? Oh I'm glad you're safe. What did you do? How did it happen? Are you hurt? There's a cut in your hair – it's bleeding a bit…nothing much. Oh Peter, it was a cruel joke! I've been crying so, ever since we said goodbye. I am crying. I had lost you for ever. Oh Peter.

PETER: I don't know. I just don't know. I should be dead. My head feels funny. I wasn't joking. Don't cry, June darling. Either life or death shall thereby be the sweeter.

They kiss and cry, cry and kiss, tears and saliva become indistinguishable. They hold on to each other, to life, to hope, to flesh and sex and earthly simplicity. The reaction is instant and chemical; relief and fear banish boundaries. They never want to let go. This is the moment. This is the prize.

SCENE 4
CHIEF RECORDER'S OFFICE

RECORDER: The case is not so simple.

CONDUCTOR: No?

RECORDER: No. He has fallen in love.

CONDUCTOR: Oh!

RECORDER: It complicates things.

CONDUCTOR: True, madame.

RECORDER: You must do your best. You will proceed to Earth immediately.

CONDUCTOR: Yes, madame.

RECORDER: You will explain your grave error to Squadron Leader Carter and ask him to accompany you back here.

A member of the crowd mutters 'bag of milk' under their breath, much to the amusement of all but the RECORDER and the CONDUCTOR.

(*To BOB.*) Your captain is not an unreasonable man, I hope?

BOB: No! ma'am. Give him my best…sir.

CONDUCTOR: With pleasure.

The screen fills with rhododendrons. We are on Earth.

SCENE 5
THE GARDEN OF RHODODENDRONS

In the garden, PETER and JUNE relax.

Song

PETER: (*Sings.*) Am I sleeping?
    Let me carry on sleeping
    Under the starlight of your eyes.

Take this moment
Safely into your keeping
Sealed with kisses soft as butterflies.

Here in your arms I'm living again,
The fears and glories and pain are gone;
Here by your side I'm breathing again,
This new world is where we belong.

Are you sleeping?
Carry on your sleeping
Under the starlight of my eyes.
I'll take this moment
Safely into my keeping
Sealed with kisses soft as butterflies.

Here in your arms I'm living again… (*Etc.*)

PETER: (*Speaks.*) Even if I had ruby slippers I wouldn't want to tap my heels together. I don't want to go home. I want to stay here.

JUNE: Then you will. For as long as you want to.

PETER: Would you like another drink?

The CONDUCTOR appears and freezes time.

CONDUCTOR: How do you do?

PETER: How do *you* do? I say, June! Wake up!

CONDUCTOR: She cannot wake. We are talking in space, but not in time.

Look at your watch.

It has stopped. PETER shakes it.

It has not moved since the moment when you said so charmingly, 'Fancy a drink.' Nor will it move until we finish our little talk.

PETER: Who are you?

CONDUCTOR: I am Conductor 71, Magnus the Magnificent – (*PETER interrupts at this point.*) – world renowned magician, illusionist and escapologist

PETER: What do you want?

CONDUCTOR: We should have met yesterday at 4:10. I bring you 'the best' from Bob Trubshaw. Would you like a bonbon?

PETER: Bob? Bob's dead.

CONDUCTOR: Aha! You are picking up the wool, as we say in Norway. And how did he die?

PETER: Cannon-shell.

CONDUCTOR: Very good. And what happens to a man who jumps from his aircraft without a parachute?

PETER: How do you know that?

CONDUCTOR: It's my job. Please answer my question. What happens to a man –

PETER: No! What do you mean it's your job?

CONDUCTOR: I'm asking the questions! Your time was up but I missed you, all because of your ridiculous English climate. I am from Norway.

PETER: Thank you very much… And goodbye. June!

No response from JUNE.

What do you want now?

CONDUCTOR: You, my friend.

PETER: What for?

CONDUCTOR: To conduct you –

PETER: Where to?

CONDUCTOR: To the training centre –

PETER: Training, for what?

CONDUCTOR: For another world –

PETER: You don't mean –

CONDUCTOR: But, my dear friend, of course that is what I mean. You should be dead. That is where I am taking you.

PETER: But I'm not dead.

CONDUCTOR: But you should be. Your time was up yesterday.

They begin to leave together.

PETER: What about her?

CONDUCTOR: Charming… You'll see her again when her time comes. She'll live to be 97. I looked her up in the files.

PETER: No. No. I'm in love with her *now*!

CONDUCTOR: But, my friend – what is love? The feeling of a moment.

PETER: I am not interested in your opinions of love. I'll make my own mind up about that – and about what happens to a man who falls out of an aeroplane for that matter.

In this case I'll tell you what happens. He meets the woman he's been looking for all his life and falls in love.

I don't care if I should have died yesterday. Yesterday I wasn't in love. Today I am.

CONDUCTOR: But how many people are in love when they die, my friend? How many? Soldiers? Airmen? How many sailors? All of them. Do they protest when their time is up? They don't.

Did I complain when my time came, drowning in a bag of milk in the Empress Theatre in Fredrikstad Sarpsborg in front of fifteen hundred people – including my own mother, watching me onstage for the first time – (*PETER interrupts at any point after this.*) – after resisting my career choice for eleven years, finally she was on the point of accepting me for what I am… (*Etc.*)

PETER: I have fallen in love because of your mistake. I'm in an entirely different position from last night. I expected to die, I was ready to die. It's not my fault that I didn't. It's yours!

CONDUCTOR: Please come with me. Please. I am in big trouble.

PETER: No.

CONDUCTOR: I am representing the eternal law of this world and the Other.

PETER: Yes. But law is based on reason.

What laws govern the country you come from? There must be a right to appeal.

CONDUCTOR: It has never been done.

PETER: Is that a reason why it can't be done now?

CONDUCTOR: You are determined to get me into – into the shit.

PETER: What about the shit you got me into?

CONDUCTOR: I'm going to have to use some special skills. I will turn you into a squirrel. Put you into my pocket and take you with me! Watch my fingers.

PETER: What are you doing?

CONDUCTOR: Look! Look at your little squirrel ears and your big bushy squirrel tail.

PETER: I haven't got ears or a tail.

CONDUCTOR: I don't understand you. You are talking squirrel language.

PETER: I've had enough of this.

PETER makes to attack the CONDUCTOR.

CONDUCTOR: I think I'll leave you for a little while. I shall report for instructions.

PETER: Go!

CONDUCTOR: I will make myself invisible and time will start to run again.

Flourish.

PETER: I can still see you.

CONDUCTOR: Really?

Look over there.

The CONDUCTOR exits. JUNE wakes up.

JUNE: Go on then.

PETER: 'Go on then' what?

JUNE: To the drink. You just asked me to have a drink.

PETER: Did I? Yes. I remember. I did.

He looks at his watch. It is ticking again.

What's the matter with me?

JUNE: What is it?

PETER: I don't know.

JUNE: You do know. Tell me why you're frightened. Peter. What's wrong?

PETER: An odd thing happened while you were asleep.

JUNE: I haven't been asleep. What happened?

PETER: I was afraid you'd say that. Did you hear us talking?

JUNE: No. Who was there to talk to?

PETER: They sent somebody.

JUNE: They? Who are they? Who did they send?

PETER: I don't know… Please. Do I look mad?

JUNE: No. Are you?

PETER: There was a ten-tenths fog last night…that's true, isn't it?

JUNE: You know there was.

PETER: And I did bale out without a parachute.

JUNE: Yes!

PETER: So how can I be alive?

JUNE: I don't know…

PETER struggles against a surge of pain in his head.

…and I don't care!

PETER: I had no parachute. It was shot up. When I came to this morning I had no parachute. Anyway, why wasn't I drowned?

JUNE: I don't care. I heard you die and then I found you alive. That's all that matters.

PETER: According to this chap, you shouldn't have –

JUNE: What chap?

PETER: This – Conductor chap – that they sent after me. He says he missed me in the fog. I didn't go with him, June. I told him I wanted to appeal. He's gone to get instructions.

It's not my fault I wasn't killed! It's not my fault I found you and fell in love with you!

PETER is overcome by the pain.

JUNE: What is it?

PETER: Nothing. I've got a headache. I – (*He cries out.*) – June! You're there, aren't you?

JUNE: Yes, Peter, of course I'm here.

PETER: I thought I'd lost you!

JUNE: You've only just found me.

SCENE 6

THE CAMERA OBSCURA

DR FRANK REEVES is in his camera obscura looking at the village. It is dark.

DOC: Nice day. 0800 hours. Temperature 58 degrees. Wisteria is out. Blossom still hanging in Mrs Seddon's orchard.

Ducks.

Phil McEwen driving to the infirmary at 11 miles an hour. Thank God I can't hear him singing.

Start of the cycling season. There goes Beverly to get the rations. Off the bike. Stands it up. And that tell-tale half-rotation of the right ankle. She's thinking about Matt.

Ed is late for work at the butcher's shop. Mrs Treadway shouting at him. She burns disappointment like the rest of us burn coal.

There's Christine Atkins waiting for the postman. Still as a heron. Her boy will never come home.

No. No post.

June. 'She walks in beauty like the night.' Only she's cycling and it's broad daylight.

Come on up!

JUNE: Hello Frank

DOC: Hello June. Come in. Shut the door.

JUNE: Surveying your kingdom?

DOC: A village doctor needs to know everything. You'd be surprised how many diagnoses I've formed up here. Not so many since there's been a black-out.

JUNE: I love looking at the world from here. It looks so different.

DOC: You see it all at once and clearly, as in a poet's eye.

There's Martin Andrews off to find driftwood on the beach.
The fire in a sailor's belly will always take him to the sea.

'I shall go the way of the open sea,
To the lands I knew before you came,
And the cool ocean breezes shall blow from me
The memory of your name.'

JUNE: I want to talk to you.

DOC: So you said on the phone. But it's really none of my
business.

JUNE: Don't be like that, Frank. Doctor McEwen says it's right
up your street.

DOC: This is my street, a village street; and I'm a village doctor.

JUNE: Only because you choose to be. Doctor McEwen says
that what you don't know about neurology would fit inside
a peanut.

DOC: I'm a good guesser.

JUNE: And your guesses are published by the Royal Society of
Medicine. Doctor McEwen says –

DOC: I know what Doctor McEwen says. I had a talk with him
on the phone yesterday evening.

JUNE: Oh, did you?

DOC: After I talked to you. This is really an RAF case. Carter
was supposed to rejoin his station in Lincolnshire today.

JUNE: I know.

DOC: And anyway what's it got to do with you?

We'll come back to that – but he's still an RAF case.

JUNE: He's not a case at all, Frank. He's a person! A – a very
fine person! And – I want you to see him, Frank. I don't
want just anybody pawing him about and asking him
questions. I want you. (*Pause.*) I'm sure that the RAF would
say that –

DOC: I know what the RAF would say. I've spoken to them too – I spoke to his commanding officer…

JUNE: Oh, Frank!

DOC: …and I spoke to his Group Medical Officer after that. Fortunately he's heard of me.

JUNE: Oh, Frank! (*She kisses him.*)

DOC: If you'd done that earlier I would have told you earlier.

JUNE: Frank. I've fallen in love. I'm in love as deep as the sea.

They are close together in the darkened room.

DOC: I'm pleased for you.

He moves to the door and then the shutters, opening them. Light rushes in and they are revealed as mortals.

But you can't kidnap injured RAF officers, just because you like the look of them.

JUNE: It happened before I saw him. I don't even think it was his voice - although that was all I had of him. It was him.

DOC: Does he still believe he baled out without a parachute?

JUNE: Yes.

DOC: And he has – curious experiences.

JUNE: Yes.

DOC: He sees things?

JUNE: And hears things.

DOC: Alright.

I'll come and see him today.

JUNE: Thank you, Frank.

He is letting her out of the door when she turns back to him.

He said he had a visitor.

DOC: Where from?

JUNE: I don't know. He said it was a Conductor from the world of the dead.

DOC: Did you tell him he was talking rubbish?

JUNE: No.

DOC: Quite right.

JUNE: He's not talking rubbish. He's talking logically.

DOC: Then he can't be in love.

They laugh. He shuts the door then opens it again.

SCENE 7

THE CONVALESCENT HOSPITAL

DR McEWEN is taking a rehearsal of A Midsummer Night's Dream.

McEWEN: To your positions! To your positions. Don't flap around like a lot of sick moths. Forget the grubby walls of our hospital. They are vanished. We are in a magical forest. The forest of Shakespeare's *Midsummer Night's Dream.*

Shakespeare – Shakespeare is the balm of hurt minds. That's what Shakespeare is.

The rhythm. The metre. The poetry. The passion. The landscape of the dream.

Work your imaginations! There is such a thing as the sheer force of poetry.

I remember watching this play as a child. I can't have been more than seven or eight years old. It was soon after the war. Jack Buchanan was in it, I think. I remember it as being Boxing Day – which is probably wrong. But that's how I remember it. I can picture the fairies most of all, and in the cloakroom, at the end of the show, I remember seeing a twig under the door. And the woman I was with, who wasn't my mother, said it was a fairy's foot. I took it home and kept it.

Come on! Act Three Scene One.

To your positions. Titania asleep. Enter Bottom. Sergeant Bellamy –

BELLAMY: I don't want to do it.

McEWAN: This is a play. You are not Sergeant Bellamy. Your crew is not dead. This is not a hospital. You are Bottom the Weaver and you are about to fall in love with the Queen of the Fairies.

BELLAMY: Yes doctor.

McEWAN: Go! Bray! Sergeant Bellamy. Be Bottom. Be Bottom!

BELLAMY: 'Ee-aw! Ee-aw! Hee-haw!'

NURSE: (*Playing Titania.*) 'What angel wakes me from my flowery bed?'

BELLAMY: 'Hee-haw! Hee-haw!'

Enter PETER and JUNE.

NURSE: 'I pray thee, gentle mortal, sing again.
Mine ear is much enamour'd of thy note:
So is mine eye enthralled to thy shape;
And thy fair virtue's force, perforce, doth move me,
On the first view, to say, to swear, I love thee.'

BELLAMY: 'Hee-haw!'

NURSE: 'Pease-blossom! Cobweb! Moth! And Mustardseed!'

NURSES: 'Ready!'

NURSE: 'Be kind and courteous to this gentleman.
Feed him with apricocks and dewberries.
And pluck the wings from painted butterflies
To fan the moonbeams from his sleeping eyes.'

BELLAMY is lulled to sleep by the fairies. 'Sleep, Bottom sleep'.

35

DOC enters. He starts the band swinging and explodes with song. He is charismatic and alone. His energy fills the room.

Song

DOC: (*Sings.*) When you laugh I can't help laughing,
  When you grin my cheeks are grinning,
  When you move I can't help moving:
      I think I must be your shadow.
  When you smile I can't help smiling,
  When you dance my legs start dancing,
  If you cried I'd soon be crying:
      I think I must be your shadow.

  I remember the day that you kissed me,
      I was kissing you back for a week.
  You laughed and your laughter released me,
      You spoke and I started to speak

The AIRMEN and NURSES dance a Bacchic dance of relief and hope, the DOC their Dionysus. He winds them up like clockwork devils and watches with delight as they dance their troubles away.

JUNE dances with DOC.

When you laugh I can't help laughing,
When you grin my cheeks are grinning,
When you move I can't help moving:
    I think I must be your shadow.

Breathless, the dance ends, and a spent but peaceful atmosphere among the AIRMEN is restored. They get back into their beds and smoke woodbines.

DR McEWEN sits with BELLAMY, rehearsing his lines with him.

PETER: You must be Doctor Reeves

JUNE: (*To McEWEN.*) Thank you. (*To FRANK.*) Hello Frank. Squadron Leader Carter – Doctor Reeves.

DOC / PETER: How do you do?

DOC: Do I get some tea?

JUNE: It's ordered. Ginger Snaps.

DOC: Who's winning?

JUNE: Peter's very good.

PETER: But she's winning.

JUNE: I've told Peter.

DOC: What?

JUNE: Who you are. And what you are. All about you.

DOC: I don't expect that took long.

JUNE: And I've told you all about him.

DOC: Has she read your poems?

PETER: I don't know.

JUNE: What poems?

DOC: Don't you know this is the *Peter Carter.*

JUNE: I didn't know.

PETER: We hadn't got around to that.

DOC: 'Your hair explicable as a waterfall
in some black liquid cooled by legend
fell across my thought in a moment
became a garment I am naked without'

I haven't got much modern stuff in my library but you're
there.

PETER: Good.

DOC: Now let's get down to this thing. You never had any
visions or hallucinations before?

PETER: Never.

DOC: What were you in civil life?

PETER: I was at Oxford.

DOC: Both parents alive?

PETER: My mother.

DOC: Brothers? Sisters?

PETER: Two sisters. Both in the Wrens.

DOC: What was the cause of your father's death?

PETER: Same as mine. (*Grins at JUNE.*)

DOC: Brain?

PETER: No. War.

DOC: When.

PETER: 1917.

JUNE listens. She is hearing all this for the first time.

DOC: Called up?

PETER: Volunteered. Trained in Canada. Went on ops in '41.

DOC: You must have done a good many operations.

PETER: Sixty-seven.

DOC: A survivor.

PETER: Yes.

BELLAMY is being rehearsed by McEWEN.

BELLAMY: 'I have had a dream past the wit of man to say what dream it was. Man is but an ass if he go about t'expound this dream. Methought I was…and methought I had…'

DOC: These headaches – where do they occur?

PETER: Here – and here.

DOC: Frontal and temporal. Did you have any of these symptoms before the accident?

PETER: No.

DOC: Any bang on the head?

PETER: Only whatever happened in the aircraft.

DOC: Hmm.

PETER: Does that spoil everything?

DOC: No. (*Smiles.*) These headaches, have they been getting worse?

PETER: Yes.

DOC: Do you mind if I try something?

PETER: Go ahead.

> *DOC places himself directly behind PETER so that they have exactly the same field of vision.*

DOC: Don't move your eyes. Look straight ahead.

PETER: Check.

DOC: What are you looking at?

PETER: That woman in the black dress.

DOC: Right. I've got her. Don't take your eyes off her.

PETER: Okay.

DOC: Without moving your eyes – what can you see on the extreme right?

PETER: A man dressed as a donkey.

DOC: In the centre.

PETER: Woman in black.

DOC: Extreme left?

PETER: (*Not so glib.*) Windows.

DOC: Curtains.

PETER: Yes.

DOC: Colour?

PETER: Red.

They are yellow.

DOC: You can move your eyes now.

DOC is confident. He knows what he's dealing with. PETER appears nonchalant.

PETER: Who is she?

JUNE: A visitor? I don't know.

PETER cannot help stealing a glance at the curtains.

DOC: Yes. They're yellow curtains.

PETER: Hmm.

DOC: And you've – seen something?

PETER: Someone.

DOC: Clearly?

PETER: As clear as I see you.

DOC: Hmm. Tell me, do you believe in the survival of human personality after death?

PETER: Yes I do. I thought you said you'd read my verses.

DOC: (*To JUNE.*) Do you?

JUNE: No. I don't.

PETER: (*To the DOC.*) Do you?

DOC: I don't know. I think the human personality is remarkably resiliant and I know the little bone shell it lives in moderately well. But as for what happens to it after you die…

I thought I was asked to tea.

JUNE: It's coming.

DOC: One last question. It may sound silly but…have you smelt anything recently that couldn't possibly be there?

PETER: Yes. I thought it was silly. I would never have told you.

DOC: It's important. It might help to explain everything that you've seen and heard.

PETER: That would be a relief. But it wouldn't explain how I could jump without a parachute and still be alive.

DOC: No, it couldn't do that. But there might be a practical explanation even of that.

Now this visitor – you saw him quite clearly.

PETER: I told you: as clear as I see you.

DOC: And the smell. Was it at the same time?

PETER: Yes. It was particularly strong.

DOC: Could you place it?

PETER: Oh, yes. Burnt toast.

BELLAMY: 'Thus die I, thus, thus, thus.
    Now am I dead,
    Now am I fled;
    Now soul is in the sky;
    Tongue, lose thy light
    Moon, take thy flight
    Now die, die, die, die, die.'

WOMAN: It's alright. It's alright.

DOC: Now, this messenger – he hasn't turned up again.

PETER: No, but he will.

DOC: When?

PETER: He picks his own moment and freezes time.

JUNE: Peter lodged an appeal.

DOC: Against what?

JUNE: To fight for the right to live.

DOC: That's the spirit. Don't give in.

JUNE: He won't.

PETER: I won't.

DOC: I've got bad news for you.

JUNE: Then why the grin?

DOC: He's coming with me.

JUNE: Where to?

DOC: To my house. For two reasons. First, I want to meet this chap next time he drops in.

Second, I like a nice girl around the house and she only comes to see me to borrow a book; and she's a slow reader.

With you staying, she'll be there at the end of every shift.

PETER: What about my CO? I should get back to my station.

DOC: I've fixed it with him. Besides, until we get this settled, I am your CO.

And at my house you'll get your tea at half past four.

JUNE: Thanks Frank. I've got to get ready for my shift. Bye bye.

PETER: Thank you for coming, Doctor Reeves. I'm lucky that June knew you.

DOC: June has lucky friends.

The scene transforms into the Doctor's House.

Simultaneously, JUNE is on the airwaves talking to landing pilots.

Pauses between lines for replies etc.

JUNE: Hello T Tommy. Control answering. Okay to taxi up the runway and take off, point 3, over.

Hello P Peter. Control answering. No. Stand by. Over.

Hello R Robert. Okay to taxi out. Keep clear of the runway and take off after T Tommy. Over.

Hello K Kitty from Control, turn 3, fifteen hundred feet, over.

Hello G George, Control answering. Message received and understood. Taxi back as quickly as possible and keep clear of the runway as there are aircraft about to take off, over.

Hello R Robert. You may take off now, over.

Control to Zebra, receiving you strength 5 over. Hello P Peter, Control calling, come in and land, over.

Hello K Kitty, Control calling, turn to land number 2, is this understood, over?

Hello F Freddie, Control answering. No, stand by. There is an aircraft landing over.

SCENE 8
DOC'S LIBRARY

PETER is lying asleep on a couch surrounded by books. The DOC and JUNE are playing table tennis in the open courtyard next door.

Song

Hold out your hand and I'll touch it,
Trust me. It isn't a dream.
If you've got the heart to believe it,
Things can be more than they seem

Can your hear that music in the distance?
Listen and you'll recognise the theme.
If you've got the heart to believe it
Things can be more than they seem.

(You said)
Only believe that the clouds are high
Only believe that the sky is blue
Only believe and you'll wonder why
You didn't believe I'd come back to you.

I looked into your eyes as you left me,
I kept looking after you had gone
Cos I've got the heart to believe it.
I'll keep looking: I don't care how long.

And everything I look at seems to tell me
You're coming back to me where you belong
Cos I've got the heart to believe it.
I'll keep looking: I don't care how long.

Only believe that the clouds are high... (Etc.)

*JUNE serves. They have an excellent rally. A long and very athletic
one. They are both very keen to win. Finally she wins the point
with a curving smash.*

JUNE: I wonder if Peter's a good player.

DOC: You can ask him when he wakes up.

JUNE: He's been asleep for two and half hours.

DOC: He'll wake at eleven. My serve. 22–21.

He wants to play. She doesn't get ready.

JUNE: How do you know?

DOC: I gave him a tablet.

JUNE: Well, tell me something about him.

DOC: Are we playing table tennis or are we –

JUNE: Alright. You serve.

He does. She ignores it completely.

(*Coolly.*) Your game.

DOC: Or Peter's game.

JUNE: Now tell me what you think about him.

DOC: I think he's fascinating.

JUNE: So do I.

DOC: Not biologically – medically.

JUNE: Frank.

DOC: Have a drink?

He pours her a drink. They go over to see PETER. JUNE looks at the books.

JUNE: What do the books say, Doc?

DOC: That one won't tell you anything useful. It's my book about Jazz.

JUNE: Do you know what's wrong with him?

DOC: Yes. I think I do.

JUNE: Is he – going to be alright?

DOC: He'll be alright. Here's your drink.

JUNE: Will he have any more hallucinations?

DOC: Yes.

JUNE: How do you know?

DOC: Because this Conductor promised to come back.

JUNE: Will that make him worse?

DOC: Why should it? Now I'm not going to tell you any more.

JUNE: Do you know more? (*Pause.*) I'm going to go back to the beach – in case there's anything that might give us a clue.

DOC: You're more help to him here. The most important thing now is for him to win his case.

JUNE: You're not serious?

DOC: Perfectly serious. And we must help him to win it.

JUNE: How?

DOC: It depends what message the Conductor brings.

JUNE: What he brings? If Peter's in danger, we can't sit here waiting for a message from someone who doesn't exist. That's not exactly scientific, is it Frank?

DOC: Science is based on observation. And in medical science your best witness is the patient. In this case he's our only witness. I'd like to know who else you'd want me to listen to.

JUNE: What if it's bad news? What if the Conductor won't let him appeal? What if he loses his case? Oh! This is absurd!

DOC: It isn't absurd to him.

What he imagines is far more important than what you or I think. Look. You see that floor-board you're standing on. If I asked you to walk along it towards me without falling off, you could do it, couldn't you?

JUNE: Yes.

DOC: But if I took the same board and placed it across the top of a huge canyon – what about then?

JUNE: I don't know.

DOC: You'd be frightened because you would imagine falling to your death and you would feel in danger.

That's what Peter feels like when he imagines losing his case – and it makes curing him very difficult. Anything we can do to win his case will make him feel safer and give us more time and opportunity to make him better.

Don't worry. We will help him and he'll win.

Another game? We can't count the last one.

JUNE: I can't.

DOC: Don't worry about him. See that bell?

JUNE: Yes.

DOC: He's promised to ring it if he gets another visit.

JUNE: Come on then.

DOC: You serve. You're still up by five games to two but this is the start of my come-back.

In mid-shot, the world stands still and PETER sits up, stirs and sniffs. He sniffs again. He sits up quickly.

PETER sees the CONDUCTOR and tries to ring the bell. They look at the frozen game of table tennis.

PETER: Oh no! Doc! June!

CONDUCTOR: Again, we are in space but not in time.

This looks good. *Ragtime, Jazz and the Birth of Swing*, by Frank Reeves. What is a Jazz?

PETER: It's a kind of music. It came before swing. It's the doctor's book. You know – Louis Armstrong?

CONDUCTOR: Is he dead?

PETER: No. What about King Oliver?

CONDUCTOR: Of course. King Oliver, yes?

He plays the trumpet.

He is a very good friend of mine.

PETER: Really? What a feller.

CONDUCTOR: You could meet him if you want.

PETER: I'd love to. So would the Doc.

CONDUCTOR: You can meet anyone you like if you come with me. King Oliver, Helen of Troy, Mick the Midget.

PETER: Good.

CONDUCTOR: You mean you'll come.

PETER: I mean you've got good news for me.

CONDUCTOR: What do you mean?

PETER: You wouldn't try to entice me with Helen of Troy and Mick the Midget if you had the right to conduct me anywhere.

CONDUCTOR: Alright. I give up. I have good news for you.

PETER: Good!

CONDUCTOR: You are to be allowed to appeal.

PETER: Splendid!

CONDUCTOR: The trial is tomorrow.

PETER: Better and better!

CONDUCTOR: Now all you have to do is choose your counsel.

PETER: Counsel?

CONDUCTOR: To help you make the argument you should live when so many other people have died. It's going to be tricky.

PETER: Can I choose anyone?

CONDUCTOR: Anyone dead. Mick the Midget is very clever. And he's free.

PETER: Go away.

CONDUCTOR: Can I borrow this book?

PETER: No! Put it down!

CONDUCTOR: Who is Frank Reeves?

PETER: He's my doctor. I said get out.

CONDUCTOR: Or I could turn you into a periwinkle and you could hide in the sea. Watch my fingers. Watch my fingers.

PETER: Don't try that nonsense again!

CONDUCTOR: Okay I'm going. She's pretty. Do you like her?

PETER: I lost her.

CONDUCTOR: You know what they say about her? She is the village scooter.

PETER: Get out of here now now NOW!

He disappears. The table tennis game is able to resume. PETER rings the bell. This time it rings. DOC and JUNE come racing through.

JUNE: Where is he?

PETER: Didn't you see him?

DOC: He was here? He tricked us!

JUNE: What happened? What did he say?

DOC: I hope you didn't give in to anything.

PETER: Frank.

DOC: Yes?

PETER: I need to be near these books. I have to prepare my case. Can I sleep here?

DOC: Of course you can.

(*To JUNE.*) Keep him calm.

DOC goes out. PETER is upbeat but feverish.

PETER: June. I'm feeling much better. I've had some very good news.

JUNE: What, Peter.

PETER: I'm to be allowed to appeal.

JUNE: That's fantastic

PETER: If I can find a good Counsel.

JUNE: Counsel?

PETER: To defend me at my appeal.

JUNE: Of course you will. What did he say, the Conductor?

BELLAMY walks into the study and sits down.

PETER: What's he doing here?

JUNE can't see BELLAMY. She sees PETER wave at nothing.

JUNE: Where? Is he here again?

PETER realises this is something different.

PETER: No. No. The Conductor's gone. June?

The man. The pilot in the hospital with the donkey's ears.

JUNE: Why are you talking about him?

PETER: Is he dead?

DOC: I'll phone the hospital.

Perhaps BELLAMY has a rope around his neck. Or a piece of flex.

PETER: I see.

BELLAMY: Is that Doctor Reeves?

PETER: Yes.

PETER is scared. He realises that he is getting closer to death.

I don't think there's much time.

It's very important I find a good counsel.

BELLAMY: What date is it?

PETER: May the 4th.

BELLAMY: Oh that's alright then. I've got plenty of time.

JUNE: Peter. Can you hear me? Peter. Frank! Nobody can take you from me. I won't let them.

PETER: It won't be any use. A judgment against me would be backed up by all the power of this world – and of the other.

JUNE: But they won't judge against you. Frank!

She leaves to find DOC. PETER looks at BELLAMY.

PETER: What happened to you?

BELLAMY: I gave up. Couldn't face the day.

PETER: What did you fly?

BELLAMY: Wellingtons.

PETER: Flying Cigars.

BELLAMY: Yes. We were hit on the way back from Cologne. Heavy fireworks.

PETER: I heard.

BELLAMY: It was my fault. Should have seen the flaming onions. Every man in my crew was killed. I talked to them all the way home. Even though I knew they were dead. Eleven hours it took. I almost couldn't bring myself to land.

PETER: I'm sorry.

BELLAMY: We're all dead now. What did you fly?

PETER: Lancasters. Three of mine got out I think.

BELLAMY: Good for you.

JUNE and DOC re-enter, seeing PETER talking to thin air.

DOC: Lie down.

PETER: Good Lord…

DOC: What's wrong?

PETER: He took your book on Jazz.

JUNE: What?

DOC: Are you sure?

DOC crawls around looking for it on the floor.

PETER: Perfectly. He had it in his hand. What cheek!

DOC: Lie down.

PETER: Look here! You two don't believe a word of what I'm saying.

JUNE: Of course we do!

PETER: It's about my counsel.

DOC: My dear friend, here on Earth I'm your Defending Counsel. And as your counsel I believe everything you tell me.

(*To JUNE.*) There. Asleep. June. We're starting to run short of time.

JUNE: That book was there Frank? And he knew about that poor pilot who hanged himself in the hospital this morning. How did he know that?

DOC: I don't know. He won't wake for several hours. I'm going straight to the hospital.

He goes. BELLAMY sits on PETER's bed with a book of poems.

BELLAMY: 'Now in my dial of glass appears
the soldier who is going to die.'

Song

BELLAMY: (*Sings.*) When I was living, all the world was gay;
A daisied carpet spread before my feet;
Life was a sing-song, a morris dance
And it was sweet.

52

When I was living, all the world laughed loud;
The birds sang songs of joy in every wood;
The grass was green, the trees were leafy-boughed.
And life was good.

Now I am dead, is all the world the same?
Do birds still sing? Does the grass still grow green?
Does smiling Nature play her age-old game
By me unseen?

Now I am dead, does all the world still smile?
Can Nature live now that my soul has fled?
Do lanes still amble mile on rolling mile?
Now I am dead?

SCENE 9

DOC rides his motorbike through the sunny country lanes. He is reckless and loves the thrill of it. He overtakes dangerously.

SCENE 10

DOC arrives at the hospital. He is met by the SISTER and DR McEWEN.

SISTER: Hello Doctor Reeves.

DOC: Good afternoon, Sister.

SISTER: We weren't expecting you. Is there anything I can do for you?

DOC: Who is the Duty Surgeon this afternoon?

McEWEN: Doctor Archer.

DOC: Good. He's a first-class neurosurgeon.

SISTER: Indeed. And a very busy one.

DOC: I need to speak to him.

McEWEN: He's operating.

ARCHER enters.

ARCHER: Hello Frank. I thought I heard your voice.

DOC: It's about Squadron Leader Carter. Deterioration all round. We ought to operate tonight.

ARCHER: That's impossible. We're swamped.

SISTER: I did try to explain.

ARCHER: I've got a full slate of patients, all injured in combat, all requiring treatment with the highest priority.

DOC: Peter was injured in combat. And I'm afraid his condition is becoming critical. Please hear me out.

ARCHER: You're sure of your diagnosis?

DOC: Almost certain. He's getting worse quickly. I think there's an intracranial haemorrhage. His delusions are worsening. He senses his own life is in danger.

ARCHER: I don't see why his opinion is suddenly important.

McEWEN: The power of the mind, Doctor Archer. Think of the poets. 'The lunatic, the lover and the poet are of imagination all compact.'

DOC: Thank you, Doctor McEwen. He believes that his trial is fixed for tonight and he hasn't found anyone to defend him yet.

ARCHER: You talk about his hallucinations as if they were fact.

DOC: All I am saying is that his hallucinations and my diagnosis point to the same conclusion.

He thinks he will die if he loses his case. I diagnose a haemorrhage which requires immediate operation – and that's why I think we have to operate tonight.

ARCHER: We'll send an ambulance this evening. If there's any further deterioration, let us know immediately.

DOC: Thank you, Doctor Archer.

SCENE 11
THE BEACH

JUNE is walking along the beach, scouring it for evidence. Perhaps she finds a coin. Perhaps she flips it.

Song

MUSICIANS: (*Sing.*) What would I do
    If I'd never kissed you?
    Would I feel blue
    If that day I'd missed you?
    Or would I just have carried on the same as ever?

    In a single hour
    You permanently changed me;
    I was a flower,
    You picked and rearranged me;
    There's no way to carry on the same as ever.

SCENE 12
THE ESCALATOR

The CONDUCTOR enters with PETER and begins to hoist him towards the world of the dead. In the film this happens on a giant staircase. In our version it takes place on a rope. In your version you can do it however you like.

CONDUCTOR: Peter Peter. Well my friend, we have come to the end of the string. I've decided to be more helpful. Please hold this.

PETER: Thank you.

CONDUCTOR: I've been doing a lot of thinking. I have a beautiful suggestion for your counsel. What about Lord Byron?

PETER: A poet?

CONDUCTOR: He was a very good lover too.

PETER: Maybe… A poet's good… You *are* helping.

CONDUCTOR: You know what they say. Sometimes fortune smiles on the little fish.

PETER: I know! Of course! If I'm choosing a poet, I want the best. How stupid of me. I'll choose Shakespeare.

CONDUCTOR: A brilliant idea, but I'm afraid that won't be possible.

PETER: Why not?! You said I could have anyone who was dead. He's dead isn't he?

CONDUCTOR: Because, my dear fellow, we have just finalised our own choices. Shakespeare will be joining the prosecution bench. He cannot defend you at the same time.

PETER: I cannot be prosecuted by Shakespeare. I'm as good as dead. I'm coned. I'm for the blood wagon. I'm stuffed. I'm wrapped up. I'm shot to ribbons. I'm shot up with no parachute. I'm coned without a gooley chit.

CONDUCTOR: Do not over-react. We have chosen a good man. What you have to do is choose a good man yourself.

PETER: To argue against Shakespeare?

CONDUCTOR: Yes.

PETER: I can't.

CONDUCTOR: Then you will lose.

PETER: 'If I must die
    I will encounter darkness as a bride,
    And hug it in mine arms.'

    June.

CONDUCTOR: Of course. You could always withdraw your appeal. It's not too late for that.

PETER: Hang on! Why are you giving me all this advice? What interest have you got in my winning my case?

CONDUCTOR: I?

PETER: Yes, you! Why are you taking me up this rope? I know where this goes and it isn't to the appeal. If I die before tomorrow, that's it, isn't it? Game over. No appeal. No Life for me. No disgrace for you. You're taking me for a ride!

CONDUCTOR: What a suggestion! I give you good luck in your goblet – (*PETER interrupts at any point after this.*) – and you throw it back in my moustache!

PETER: I don't like it. I don't like your suggestions. And I don't like you. I think I'll go back before it's too late.

CONDUCTOR: Peter! Peter! Don't be a fool! We were so nearly there. Come back! You can't do this to me!

The CONDUCTOR is further and further away.

Peter! Peter! Come back! Come back!

SCENE 13
DOC'S STUDY

Rain is audible. A storm is slowly building.

JUNE: Peter! Peter! Come back! Come back!

PETER is back in the bed in the study. JUNE is with him. She is wet from the beach.

PETER: He nearly got me...

JUNE: Don't give up. Frank's been to the hospital. He's spoken to them. It's going to be alright.

PETER is in a high fever.

PETER: Find me a copy of Shakespeare, would you.

JUNE: You need to calm down Peter.

PETER: (*Fiercely.*) Just bring me the book!

JUNE: Not now.

PETER: Please. June, they've done a terrible thing. They've asked Shakespeare to prosecute me.

JUNE: It's a trick. It must be a trick.

PETER: I can't take that chance.

Get the book and read it.

Read *Romeo and Juliet*. Act Five. Scene One. 'I dreamt…'

JUNE: 'I dreamt my lady came and found me dead –
Strange dream that gives a dead man leave to think!
And breathed such life with kisses in my lips
That I revived and was an emperor.'

PETER: Good. Now Act Five Scene Three. About line ninety. 'Death, that hath sucked…'

JUNE: 'Death, that hath sucked the honey of thy breath,
Hath had no power yet upon they beauty.
Thou art not conquered. Beauty's ensign yet
Is crimson in thy lips and in thy cheeks,
And death's pale flag is not advanced there.'

PETER: But it will advance.

JUNE: Peter. This isn't helping you. It's making you worse. You have to stop! Peter!

PETER: I can't do it by myself. (*Suddenly anxious again.*) I need to find my counsel. I need to find help!

JUNE: What about me? I can help you!

PETER: You can't help me. You're not dead.

The storm, which has been building during this scene, erupts in a peal of thunder.

DOC steps forward. He has been listening.

JUNE: Why isn't the ambulance here?

DOC: It was supposed to be here half an hour ago!

JUNE: Now he thinks Shakespeare is going to prosecute him.

DOC: I need to stay with him.

Could you phone Doctor McEwen. We *must* operate tonight. It's a matter of life and death! Find out what's happened to the ambulance.

JUNE leaves.

Hello, Peter.

PETER: Where is she?

DOC: Phoning. Back in a minute.

PETER: He is a crafty beggar. I just got away, by the skin of my teeth.

DOC: I know.

PETER: They've asked Shakespeare to prosecute me. I'm done for, Doc.

DOC: Now look here, don't let anybody fool you into throwing up the case. You've been allowed to appeal.

Look at me. You are promised a fair trial. Don't give in to anybody.

Promise me.

PETER: I've got no counsel.

DOC: Don't worry. We'll find somebody.

PETER: Nobody famous, but someone with his head screwed on alright.

DOC: What about an airman?

BELLAMY: I'm an airman. I could do it.

PETER: (*To BELLAMY.*) No. Not you!

(*To DOC.*) Someone from my crew?

DOC: How about your radio operator?

PETER: Bob?

BELLAMY: Bob? All he does is eat sweets.

PETER: In the air he was a tiger and on the ground he was as soft as butter on a hot crumpet!

They fight. JUNE re-enters.

JUNE: I couldn't get through.

DOC: Perhaps it's the storm. They cut the telephones off.

BELLAMY: She's lovely. You're very lucky.

PETER: Thank you.

BELLAMY: Thank you Doctor Reeves.

PETER: He can't hear you!

DOC: Is it stopping?

There is a moment of silence.

JUNE: No. Getting worse. I'll go on my bike.

DOC: I'll go and it will be quicker. If the ambulance arrives don't wait for me. I'll meet you at the hospital.

BELLAMY: Oh that's me. I'm going with him. Wish me luck.

PETER: Where are you going?

JUNE: I'm staying here.

PETER: No the man with the ears.

No. Frank!

JUNE crosses to PETER. DOC walks out. BELLAMY walks out immediately behind him.

JUNE pulls PETER to the ground.

SCENE 14
DOC'S GARAGE

After the Doc's exit, the BOY returns to the stage with a tiny motorcycle in his hand. He narrates as he drives the bike over the prone bodies of PETER and JUNE.

BOY: Approaching midnight, May 4th.

> No pea-souper tonight. A wild storm is blowing its top.

> Hello? What's that?

> Someone wheeling a motorbike out into the sheets of rain.

> The ignition catches and the engine roars into life.

> The rider switches on the lights and drives straight out into the storm.

SCENE 15
DOC'S LIBRARY

PETER wakes. He's delirious.

PETER: Where's Frank?

JUNE: He won't be long.

PETER: I must speak to him

> What if my appeal doesn't exist? It could just be part of my sickness couldn't it?

> Well couldn't it?

JUNE: Yes it could.

PETER: I have to prepare myself for death.

JUNE: NO.

PETER: One way or the other, I am going to die and I have to get ready.

JUNE: Stop it Peter. You're turning away from me! DON'T TURN AWAY FROM ME!

PETER: I'm not. This is real. You have to accept it too, June. You have to let me go.

It will be just as we thought it was going to be. But this time when you send a telegram to my mother you'll be able to say that you really knew me.

JUNE: It's not like it was going to be, Peter. It's different. You're alive!

If you die you die. But as long as you're alive I'll keep fighting for you and you need to start fighting for me too.

PETER: You don't understand. I can't.

JUNE: You can. Promise me you'll keep fighting your appeal. You'll represent yourself if you have to. Whatever you need. For me, Peter, promise me you won't give up.

The storm erupts.

SCENE 16

DOC'S LAST RIDE

The BOY continues his narration as DOC enacts his last ride. BELLAMY rides pillion.

BOY: This rider seems to know the road blindfolded. Above him the clouds roll in from the sea. The storm is getting worse.

He drives fast, as if he knows no fear.

Hello? What's this? Flashing lights. An ambulance racing through the night to collect some pilot for a brain op. And the bike.

Like two planets on a collision course.

DOC crashes.

Look at that. A flash of flame in a vast patchwork landscape.

A thin curl of smoke climbing into the sky.

By the time the fire extinguishers have done their work it is too late.

Song

CHORUS: (*Sings.*) When you laugh I can't help laughing,
    When you grin my cheeks are grinning,
    When you move I can't help moving:
        I think I must be your shadow.
    When you smile I can't help smiling,
    When you dance my legs start dancing,
    If you cried I'd soon be crying:
        I think I must be your shadow.

    I remember the day that you kissed me,
        I was kissing you back for a week.
    You laughed and your laughter released me,
        You spoke and I started to speak.

JUNE sees that DOC is dead.

JUNE: Frank. No!

She is surrounded by the CHORUS.

Go away. Go away!

SCENE 17
THE OPERATING THEATRE

PETER is wheeled into the operating theatre, which forms around him.

The DOCTORS, SURGEONS and NURSES are preparing for the operation. There is a small crowd, for many are anxious to see this highly-skilled operation.

JUNE bursts into the ante-room.

JUNE: (*To DR McEWEN.*) Can I speak to him?

McEWEN: Go ahead. But he won't hear you.

JUNE: (*Bending over PETER.*) You can have the perfect counsel, Peter. If you want him. (*She whispers.*) Keep fighting Peter. Don't let them win.

They get PETER into position and are about to begin the operation, scalpels raised, when the CONDUCTOR enters and freezes the action.

CONDUCTOR: I'm sorry to interrupt, Peter. But the cuckoo is about go out into the moonlight.

You have to choose your counsel. They won't wait any more.

The little GIRL enters, skipping by.

PETER: Fine. Who do I report to?

SCENE 18
THE PLACE YOU GO WHEN YOU DIE

DOC and BELLAMY enter throught the audience, meeting them as they walk and chatting to them about being dead.

As they reach the stage, they continue…

DOC: Thank you very much. You've been an excellent companion.

BELLAMY: I haven't been here long. You were my first passenger. They were very clear that they weren't going to tolerate any more mistakes. I was hanging around waiting for you for days.

DOC: Well you needn't have worried.

BELLAMY: I'm still on probation.

RECORDER: Well done Conductor 42, you did very well

They stand facing the RECORDER. Both are very respectful.

PETER sits up, writes a note and makes a paper aeroplane, which he throws. It lands on the RECORDER's desk. She reads it.

Doctor Frank Reeves.

DOC: Yes.

RECORDER: You are familiar with the case of Squadron Leader Carter?

DOC: I am.

RECORDER: He has chosen you to be his counsel.

DOC: (*Smiles gently.*) I hoped he would.

RECORDER: Do you accept?

DOC: I do.

RECORDER: You have very little time to prepare your case.

The stage transforms into the Court of Appeal.

SCENE 19
THE UNIVERSAL SUPREME COURT
OF THE LIVING AND THE DEAD

Fanfare. The Court assembles. There is a long table, covered in a white tablecloth. There are nameplates and microphones, like a war crimes tribunal.

RECORDER: Ladies and Gentlemen, the court is open.

Fanfare.

Pray silence for the Judge.

JUDGE: The court of appeal sits to consider the case of Peter Carter vs The Universe.

Mister Carter claims negligence against the heavens, and superior rights and responsibilities arising from that negligence.

He claims that on 2nd May, the date that his death was registered at the department of records, he found himself miraculously alive and on earth.

CONDUCTOR: This much my Lord is beyond dispute.

JUDGE: He claims that he was perfectly reconciled to die at that point but that the moment was missed and now he deserves to live.

CONDUCTOR: That is what is in dispute.

JUDGE: It has been decided that we will hear his appeal.

Could I please see the term of his life.

Thank you.

If this appeal succeeds, I will rewrite the term of his life to balance any injustice he has suffered.

CONDUCTOR: The mist was so thick, your Honour. I couldn't see my own hair.

JUDGE: If not, his life will end forthwith.

There are many of you, due to the unusual degree of excitement about this case. Of course there is room for all who wish to attend, but we have reserved the front rows for those with a special interest in Peter Carter and his affairs.

Here are many distinguished and gallant veterans of the Great War of 1914, of the Boer War, the Crimean War, the American Civil War, the Franco-Prussian War, the Sino-Japanese War, the Boxer rebellion, the South Sea Wars, the Wars of the Dutch Indies, the Hundred Years' War, the battles of Salamis, Quebec and Antioch, the sieges of Jerusalem, Maffiking and Harfleurs…

The COMPANY list battles and wars.

My friends, the counsel for the prosecution.

*We see three people sitting at a bench: SHAKESPEARE
and FATHER (not immediately recognisable), alongside the
CONDUCTOR.*

And do we have a counsel for the defence?

DOC enters.

DOC: Now, who's in charge here?

JUDGE: I am. Please sit down for a moment Doctor Reeves.

PETER: Frank! You accepted.

DOC: I'm very flattered you asked me.

PETER: I couldn't be in better hands. Your book.

DOC: Thank you

The Court settles.

JUDGE: Ladies and gentlemen of the court, the case before us is
very simple.

Conductor 71?

CONDUCTOR: Within a few hours of stolen life, we are told
that Mister Carter has fallen in love. As if that should mean
that he –

DOC: Your Honour I object. Those few hours were not stolen.
They were given to him – by an oversight I admit – but
undoubtedly they were a gift.

JUDGE: Ladies and Gentlemen – whether or not the hours were
stolen is immaterial.

What you have to decide is far simpler than that.

Is it possible that this love – however strong or weak it is
– should prevent us from correcting the accident by which
Peter Carter escaped his own death.

Are the rules of life and death to be bent for the sake of
love?

DOC: I object!

> I agree we must prove that Peter and June are in love – and I should know that if anyone should.
>
> But we are not arguing to break a single one of your rules.
>
> That term of life you hold in your hand, my Lord, is already forfeit. Its date is past and it must be rewritten.
>
> Even if my client loses today, you will simply have to cross out the 2nd May and write the 5th.
>
> I am not arguing that Love should routinely conquer Death. That would be absurd. But in this case, Death itself has stumbled and a unique opportunity has arisen.
>
> What a chance then – for ONCE – to look at the impact that love might have upon the lives of two people – and their friends and those close to them – and to decide accordingly whether it should be allowed to flourish or not.

PETER: Well done, Frank. That was brilliant.

JUDGE: Who speaks for the prosecution?

FATHER: Ray Carter, Captain, 7th Battalion, East Surrey Infantry.

PETER: My father!

FATHER: Peter. I am sorry to see you in this terrible position.

PETER: Father. What happened to you? Why are you here?

FATHER: Your Honour. He has never met me. Do you mind?

JUDGE: By all means.

> *Peter's FATHER walks round to see PETER. They look at one another.*

FATHER: How is your mother?

PETER: She's well. I think. I haven't seen her.

FATHER: And your sisters?

PETER: They know I'm alive. They are well I think… Father. Why do you…? Why are you prosecuting me?

FATHER: Because I understand you Peter. You are facing an enormous change and you are afraid.

PETER: You died at Arras, father. Did you suffer? We never heard.

FATHER: I was afraid. We were all afraid. I was afraid of suffering, of course – we all are – but most of all I was afraid of death. The clinging cold hand of death. But I needn't have been.

Life, yours included Peter, is like a pattern of changing shape and colour. Some changes are sweet, some jagged, some improbable, some wild. But they all come, Peter, whatever we think, and the last change is always death.

Mine was violent. Yours was violent.

PETER: I am not dead, father. Why do you want me dead?

FATHER: Your death, Peter, is the very thing which will give meaning to your life and will inspire those who care for you – those you love.

He sits.

PETER: My father! It's my father. I never met him until now. You told me about Shakespeare! Why didn't you tell me about my father?

CONDUCTOR: He's your father. I thought you'd be pleased.

PETER: Why does he want me dead? Why doesn't he want me alive?

SHAKESPEARE: What do we know of the heart of a man who is yet living? It is only in death that we are truly ourselves. A prince can crumble into cowardice in the face of death. A lifelong villain can show himself a true man.

PETER: Who's that?

CONDUCTOR: Don't you recognise your favourite poet?

PETER: It isn't Shakespeare.

BELLAMY: Shakespeare?

CONDUCTOR: But of course it is.

BELLAMY: Oh my God. (*He faints.*)

PETER: Shakespeare wouldn't say that!

SHAKESPEARE: What do you expect me to do? Speak in verse?

PETER: No, but –

SHAKESPEARE: (*Furious.*) What do you know about what Shakespeare would say?! What do you know about how I died?!

RECORDER: Order!

PETER: I don't understand. How could you, who write with power about human feeling be standing there arguing against it.

BELLAMY: You're right. Tell him.

SHAKESPEARE: I am not arguing against feeling, but for it. When I lived I drank in every detail of life. I was plunged so deep in human feeling that I would have found it impossible to imagine myself standing here arguing the part of Death.

But I am not alive. I'm dead. We are all dead here.

But that doesn't means we are without feeling.

Look at this world.

How simple and strange it is. How full of variety, yet always comprehensible and orderly. It is like fiction, Peter, like poetry. Everything has found its place.

'Fear no more the heat o'the sun,
    Nor the furious winter's rages;

Thou thy worldly task hast done,
    Home art gone, and ta'en they wages;
Golden lads and girls all must,
    As chimney sweepers, come to dust.'

The CHORUS start to sing 'Sleep, Peter, sleep.'

DOC: Don't give in to him, Peter.

PETER: I'm not.

DOC: May I call a witness?

JUDGE: Of course.

RECORDER: We call Flight Lieutenant Bob Trubshaw, Peter's Sparks.

PETER: A brilliant idea.

BOB enters.

Bob! It's you.

BOB: What ho! We miss you up here, Peter.

PETER: Thanks, Bob. It's good to see you. I can't tell you how good.

BOB: I thought you'd never get here.

PETER: Here I am.

BOB: Hale and hearty.

PETER: I'm having a hell of a job fighting this case, you know.

BOB: I can see that. Chin up.

PETER: What's it like up here?

BOB: Well it's not as bad as you'd think. There's music upstairs and dancing on Tuesdays. And I never run out of these.

PETER: They're not treating you too badly, then?

BOB: Quite the opposite. There's even a bar.

PETER: Oh?

BOB: And I don't know how it happens, but I keep finding things I had as a child – like my tricycle.

PETER: And so you should!

BOB: But it's the company I like best, Peter.

We're all together up here. Ed, James, Davy. All the lads from that first raid – you remember Marcus? – when we came home – and – went to the mess – and – they weren't there. You remember?

PETER: You were a brick about that, Bob.

BOB: And the other raids after that.

PETER: Then too. Always.

BOB: Thanks.

BOB: How many raids did you do?

PETER: Sixty-seven.

BOB: A good innings.

PETER: Not out.

BOB: We're all here Peter. All of us. There's no more waiting. No more waiting.

Only trouble is there's no one in the pilot's seat.

It's the other way round now Peter. It's like we've all come home except you.

Peter.

Don't bunk out now Peter.

You're with us. Remember?

BOB starts to leave, very slowly. The music from the cockpit sequence at the start of the show begins to play.

DOC: Someone's got to him.

FATHER: No one's got to him.

PETER starts to follow them.

PETER: I'll go wherever they go.

DOC: Don't be stupid, Peter.

PETER: No Frank. He's just telling the truth. Those men are part of my life in a way June isn't.

DOC: They're dead already – in spite of your best efforts to save them. You've actually got a chance to live.

FATHER: I think Peter is ready to die.

PETER speaks to SHAKESPEARE.

PETER: 'Reason thus with life:
If I do lose thee, I do lose a thing
That none but fools would keep.'

DOC: But even when he was saying that, he was falling in love.

FATHER: He wasn't falling in love. He was desperate for any kind of feeling that's all.

PETER: I love you June. You're life but I am leaving you. Where do you live?

FATHER: We are all desperate for feeling in war, Frank. We cling to any human feeling we can. Whatever it is, love, music, poetry, a picture in our wallets. You were there too, Frank. Don't you remember?

PETER: Were you, Frank? In the First War? I didn't know.

DOC: What does it matter? You might have been desperate for feeling at first but their man lost you and your love for June grew out of it. That's what we're arguing about.

PETER: Frank. I can't go on with this. We don't have a leg to stand on. I want to withdraw the appeal.

DOC stands in PETER's way, forcibly stopping him.

DOC: We wouldn't have a leg to stand if we didn't have some evidence.

But we do.

And while we're arguing about how many angels can dance on the head of a pin, a young woman is standing in an operating theatre watching the man she loves struggling for his life under the knife of a surgeon.

My Lord. May I? Please?

JUDGE: You may.

JUNE is transported into the court room.

DOC: She's hardly left his side for days. She teases him, strengthens him, cajoles him – and he's fighting to stay alive for her sake – not to avoid death or abandon his duty. He clearly showed that by being ready to die in the first place.

We're not talking about what happened in those first moments in the cockpit. We're talking about the love that has grown since – in the time that wouldn't have existed if it wasn't for – I'm sorry my friend – a mistake which was no fault of his own.

BELLAMY: Look!

DOC: What?

BELLAMY: She's crying.

DOC: What proof of that love could you possibly want, beyond seeing the two of them and what they feel for each other?

Beyond seeing this tear on the cheek of a woman whose breaking heart is in your hands.

Would you mind?

BELLAMY takes a flower from his garland and takes the tear from JUNE's cheek.

BELLAMY: I am honoured.

BELLAMY holds up the tear.

DOC: It's a matter of belief.

Here in this tear is belief in love and truth and friendship. And that belief, if we let it, might mend this broken world.

[Here in this tear are love and truth and friendship. Those qualities alone can build a new world today and must build a better one tomorrow.]

Applause.

Thank you.

He sits.

JUDGE: So, do you want to withdraw your appeal, Mister Carter, or don't you?

PETER: Your Honour. I apologise. I do not wish to withdraw my appeal. I want June. I want to be with June. And if I have to die, I will die wanting to be with June.

JUDGE: Very well. Then we must continue.

Enter the WOMAN.

DOC: Who's she?

JUDGE: Would you mind telling Mister Carter where you're from.

WOMAN: I'm from Coventry.

DOC: Who called her?

JUDGE: Peter did.

PETER: I know Coventry. It was horribly bombed.

DOC: Peter?

WOMAN: We were bombed.

PETER: Yes. I'm sorry to hear that.

WOMAN: By a plane – like yours.

PETER: Not quite like mine. A German one I hope.

WOMAN: Yes. A German one. Are they very different from the English ones?

DOC: What do you mean? There's all the difference in the world. Our chaps were up there fighting them off –

WOMAN: Not to me there isn't.

PETER is baffled. The WOMEN OF DRESDEN stand up from the crowd. There are thousands of them. The sound of the engines start up, as from the first scene.

PETER: Who are they? They're not from Coventry too, are they?

WOMAN: No Peter. They're from Dresden, in Germany.

PETER: My God.

BOY: That point of fire is a burning city. It had a thousand-bomber raid an hour ago. And here, rolling in over the Atlantic is a real English fog. I hope all our aircraft got home safely.

JUNE'S VOICE: Request your position. Request your position.

PETER: June!

WOMAN: When you drop your bombs, you forget about them don't you Peter?

PETER: You have to. You're trained to.

BOB: I say. This is out of order.

WOMAN: Who says so?

PETER: (*To BOB.*) It's okay Bob.

(*To WOMAN.*) You'd go mad otherwise.

WOMAN: You'd go mad? What about us?

PETER: But don't you see? I don't choose where to drop the damn things.

JUNE'S VOICE: I cannot read you. Cannot read you. Request your position.

PETER: Position nil. June! Are you here somewhere? June!

WOMAN: When my house was bombed my children were in it.

PETER: I'm sorry to hear that. Look, I –

WOMAN: My husband's away in the war, like you. He's in the navy.

He hasn't turned up here yet, so he might still be alive.

PETER: Good. I hope he is!

WOMAN: So it was just me and the children in the house when the bomb came.

My little girl is eight and Jack, the baby, is one.

PETER: Look I'm sorry to hear that, I really am.

WOMAN: That's the girl. She's up here.

But Jack isn't. He's still down there.

He's alive. Just hasn't got a mother, that's all. Or a sister.

If he's lucky, he'll have a dad who's never met him at the end of the war. But he might not even have that.

PETER: 'But at my back I always hear Time's winged chariot hurrying near.' Andy Marvell. What a marvel…!

WOMAN: Don't you think they should let some of us go back instead of you?

A few of us?

One of us?

Rather than let you go back so you can enjoy falling in love?

PETER: What?

WOMAN: If the rules are to be broken WHY SHOULDN'T THEY BE BROKEN FOR US?

PETER: You're right. Some of them should go back.

Can't be helped about the parachute. I'll have my wings soon anyway, big white ones.

Bob? So long Bob. I'll see you. I'll see you.

PETER jumps.

JUNE'S VOICE: Hello. G for George. Hello, G George. Hello, G George.

DOC: Stop! We have to do something. His condition's critical.

SHAKESPEARE: He is dying. That is all.

JUNE: Peter! I love you, Peter. You're life and I'm leaving you!

SHAKESPEARE: But don't think that his love will die with him. His love and this story will live to be told again long after he is dead. It is already the perfect love story.

FATHER: Welcome home. You will soon be at peace.

DOC: Peter. Peter. Don't listen to them.

JUNE bursts into the court room.

JUNE: Enough! A life for a life. I'll take his place and you can send him back! Take me not him! Take me not him!

She mounts the escalator and starts climbing.

PETER: Stop. Stop her!

He tries to follow.

JUDGE: Restrain him!

JUNE: You're safe! You're safe Peter.

JUDGE: Stop everything!

Everything stops except JUNE running. She collapses. The escalator carries her down and slows to a halt. She is delivered at the feet of the JUDGE. PETER escapes from his restrainers and goes to her. In their unity they are oblivious of the Court.

Now. How does the Court find?

The RECORDER consults with the CHORUS.

RECORDER: For the defendant, your Honour.

Love cannot mend the horrors of the war we've fought. But if we are ever to recover our human dignity, then everyone who survives must find a still place in their heart where a new and simple love can grow.

This man and this woman have found that already.

JUDGE: Very well.

He writes a new date on the term of life and shows it to DOC.

Does this seem fair to you gentlemen?

DOC: Ample.

Goodbye Peter. Good luck. Goodbye June.

[FATHER: Goodye Peter. I wish you the best in love and life. I will want for you here.]

CONDUCTOR: Goodbye Peter. I'll get you in the end.

Magically PETER is back in the hospital, JUNE is at his bedside.

Enter DR McEWEN and MR ARCHER.

McEWEN: How is he? Were we in time?

ARCHER: His chances are about even.

The BOY takes a coin out of his pocket and flicks it in the air.

IF IT'S HEADS:

The room is a normal hospital with busy NURSES and AIRMEN recuperating. They are talking and laughing. A new emergency arrives and the medical staff immediately swing into action: saving lives is commonplace.

PETER: I won my case.

JUNE: I know.

IF IT'S TAILS:

The room is a normal hospital with busy NURSES and AIRMEN recuperating. They are talking and laughing. JUNE is sitting beside PETER's body. He is dead.

JUNE: Peter. Peter. Peter. Peter. Peter.

ARCHER: I'm sorry. We did everything we could.

POSTSCRIPT

'We, the peoples of the United Nations determined to save succeeding generations from the scourge of war, which twice in our lifetimes has brought untold sorrow to mankind, and to reaffirm faith in fundamental human rights, in the dignity and worth of the human person, in the equal rights of man and woman and of nations large and small.'

– Preamble to the *Charter of the United Nations,*
signed on 26 June 1945